T0129461

MANAGING THE MIRRORS

Practical Insights for Medical Leaders

PAUL D. VANCHIERE, MBA

authorHOUSE®

AuthorHouse™
1663 Liberty Drive
Bloomington, IN 47403
www.authorhouse.com
Phone: 1 (800) 839-8640

Published by AuthorHouse 12/29/2018

ISBN: 978-1-5462-6683-9 (sc)
ISBN: 978-1-5462-6682-2 (e)

Library of Congress Control Number: 2018913182

Print information available on the last page.

This book is printed on acid-free paper.

DEDICATION

This book is dedicated to my father, Dr. Charles "Buzzy" Vanchiere, MD, FAAP. A man of humble beginnings, Buzzy became a highly respected pediatrician in Lake Charles, Louisiana, for over 30 years. During his tenure, he was the managing partner of what was then one of the largest private pediatric practice in the state.

Through his involvement with the Louisiana State Medical Society, the Louisiana chapter of the American Academy of Pediatrics, and various volunteer posts at the national level within the American Academy of Pediatrics, Buzzy formed friendships with countless people around the country. I have had the pleasure of associating with many of these amazing people.

My father's professional motivation was finding innovative ways to ensure that people had adequate access to health care, particularly children. Whether it was testifying at state and national legislative hearings, meeting with government officials, or simply listening to families talk about their needs, Buzzy always sought to find ways to improve the health and well-being of people.

Aligned with this commitment to his patients was Buzzy's leadership in tending to the fiscal realities of running a medical practice. He believed that if pediatricians had strong financial foundations, they would be more comfortable in investing in new approaches that could improve the lives of children. In support of this belief, he worked with many of his colleagues to form a group within the American Academy of Pediatrics called the Section of Administration and Practice Management (SOAPM), which currently has over 1,400 members.

While I am humbled by SOAPM's continued commitment to honoring Buzzy's contributions to pediatric practice management since his passing in 2000, I believe his true legacy is the love he had for his wife, Donna, and their five children and 19 grandchildren. Buzzy possessed an engaging personality, and he always sought to find ways to help others excel to their highest potential. He is truly missed by many.

INTRODUCTION

Running a successful medical practice requires more than just being a talented physician: clinical skills will get one only so far. As a practitioner, one also must develop their capabilities as an effective manager and leader to bring out the best in the people with whom they work. Otherwise, their practice will never come close to reaching its fullest potential.

The good news is that this does not have to be a Herculean task, as the first step to developing your management skills is a rather simple one: just look in the mirror.

Like so many others, I learned this very simple lesson the hard way—by taking a hard look in the mirror when I *wasn't* meeting performance expectations. Relatively early in my career, I was an Office Manager for a group of pediatricians at one of 38 general pediatric locations operated by one of the premier children's hospitals in Texas. Unfortunately, my performance did not meet expectations, and I found myself facing a performance improvement plan that provided a last-ditch effort for me to step up to the responsibilities of the job I was hired to do or I would have to find other employment.

Looking in the mirror was tough. It was painful to admit that I had failed at being an effective manager, but the clarity of vision that I gained as a result of this admission helped me realize that I had a choice to make. I could choose to explain away the reasons for my poor performance and take advantage of the friendships that I had developed with the physicians and others to whom I reported. However, that would not have been fair to them. They needed someone to manage the practice and to help them thrive. So, instead, I decided to follow their plan for improving my performance, and in the process, I proved that I was capable and committed to succeeding—so much so that despite my prior shortcomings, I was later selected to be part of the team that provided financial analytic services for over 200 general pediatricians in the organization.

The most beneficial part of the performance improvement plan was not the actual steps in the process, but the self-reflection I undertook to recognize my own shortcomings. The people I reported to held up a mirror that provided feedback on my performance and to set clear expectations for improvement, and then gave me the space to realize what I needed to do to become an effective leader. Looking in the mirror during that performance improvement plan and managing what I learned about myself from the reflection that I saw there were essential for me to learn, grow, and demonstrate that I was now ready and able to contribute in a positive way.

In the decade since, I've carried the experience of growing professionally from the feedback of others and my own journey of self-reflection into my consulting work with dozens of medical practices around the country. Day in and day out, I work with physicians and medical practice managers to improve their financial and operational performance. Invariably, this involves helping them to look in that same mirror that I looked in so many years ago in order to assess where they can improve and develop the leadership insights and management skills needed for their employees and their practices to thrive.

Purpose of This Book

I've drawn from these past experiences to develop an approach to leadership development and strengthening management skills that explores how to manage the many mirrors that provide information about us as individuals and our practice.

In this book, I provide strategies that will help you to:

- Discover how to clearly see the blind spots and problems that currently limit your leadership and management potential

- Develop strategies to make the necessary improvements to address those problems

- Use what you see in the mirror to improve yourself, your staff, your boss (if you have one), your partner(s), your practice, and, most importantly, your patients' overall experience.

As a supplement to this book, several resources are provided on the website www.ManagingTheMirrors.com. There, you can download worksheets and activities that will help you on your journey to "Managing the Mirrors."

At the end of the day, learning how to manage the mirrors will provide insights that will help you put your best foot forward as a leader, position your team and practice for success, and provide the best possible care to your patients. I wish you all the best on your leadership journey.

CHAPTER 1

Mirror, Mirror on the Wall: What We Can Learn When We Know Where to Look

Mirrors are ubiquitous in our lives, and we find them in almost every sphere of our existence. We encounter them in bathrooms, in the bedroom, and along the walls of passageways. We use them in motor vehicles, they are a permanent fixture in department stores, and no optometrist's office would be complete without an array of them.

We even encounter mirrors in the fairy tales of our childhood. Many of us likely remember Snow White and the Seven Dwarfs. In this tale, a straight-talking mirror tells the queen that her stepdaughter Snow White is more beautiful than she is. This revelation leads to major attempts by the evil stepmother to destroy her new rival.

Much like in Snow White, mirrors can provide insights and serve several very useful physical and psychological functions in our daily lives.

- **Self-Reflection**

  A mirror provides an opportunity to see yourself and the environment around you, and to objectively assess your current state.

- **Realistic assessment**

  An objective view can provide a realistic assessment of the effort it will take to reach an intended outcome.

- **Monitoring Your Progress**

  A mirror assists in helping to check your progress toward a desired state or outcome

Not all mirrors are the same, however; nor do all of them give you the realistic view you may be looking for.

While plane mirrors (mirrors that have a flat, or planar, reflective surface, like the ones usually found in bathrooms and department stores) typically reflect objects in their realistic form without any distortion, concave or convex spherical mirrors distort the reflection of an object. This distortion is tricky. Sometimes, it can help us to see where a blind spot would otherwise be, For example, that small "blind spot mirror" I added to the side-view mirror of my family van is absolutely critical to help me spot danger and to keep my family safe. But at other times, a mirror's distortion can cause me to misjudge and see something as either larger or smaller than it actually is. Indeed, without the factory warning on my car mirror, I wouldn't know that "objects in mirror are closer than they appear."

In the same way, the size of a mirror affects what we see and how we see it. While full-length mirrors allow us to see the totality of our appearance from head to toe, smaller vanity mirrors, like the compact mirror my wife carries in her purse or the mirror on the back of the sun visor in my car allow an in-depth examination of smaller parts of ourselves. Then there's my fogless shaving mirror.: On one side, it's just a regular mirror, and I can see my whole face from a distance; on the other side, I can get a super-close view that helps me avoid cutting my face when I shave; and, thankfully, the special glass coating keeps both sides from fogging up when I shower.

I could go on, but you get the picture. Sometimes mirrors give us a realistic view, and sometimes they don't. The trick is to figure out which kind of mirror you're looking in so you know how to interpret the image it reveals and which kind of mirror you need to use when you face varied leadership and management challenges.

Using Mirrors to Improve Leadership and Practice Management

Practitioners and practice managers have many mirrors in their professional lives that they can use to assess and interpret a situation. These mirrors provide opportunities for self-reflection and progress monitoring, yet, given the nature of these instruments, they may not be as honest as the mirror is in the Snow White fairy tale.

In a typical day, you can glean information from a variety of channels on how your practice is perceived and on how your practice is performing through:

- Yourself (Self-Awareness)
- Coworkers
- Professional Colleagues
- Supervisors and Managers
- Direct Patient Feedback
- Indirect Feedback such as Body Language
- Internet-Based Reviews
- Website Rankings
- "Top Ten" Publications
- Media Reports
- Social Media
- Neighborhood Gossip
- Family
- Friends
- Gut Feelings
- A Hunch

With such an overabundance of sources for feedback, how do you decide what information is useful for further action? Additionally, what type of mirror will you use in interpreting this feedback?

Every time a physician interacts with a patient, communication takes place. Words are spoken, nonverbal cues are exchanged, and the patient forms a perception of the physician and the practice. Similarly, patients form perceptions when they interact with a medical practice. These perceptions are often shared by the patients with the rest of the world based on how the patient understood the situation. For the typical patient, all the interactions with a practice, whether they are good or unpleasant, are fair game when sharing criticism and feedback.

When faced with the daunting task of discerning which information is useful to someone, it can be easy to decide that all of the evidence at hand is coming from patients, employees, or others whose view of the situation is distorted because they cannot see the full reality of running a successful medical practice. Practice leaders may think they're looking in a full-length mirror and can see the complete picture, whereas they are actually looking in something akin to a fun-house mirror that distorts the real situation. Yet, in taking that approach, practice leaders might be misinterpreting the situation and thus missing out on critical feedback that the practice needs to act upon.

The Individual Mirror: Understanding Yourself

Surely you are familiar with the old saying that the "definition of insanity is doing the same thing repeatedly and expecting different results." So, when most rational persons want different results, they change something in their lives. They take well-reasoned actions, develop new ways of thinking, or try to build new habits.

These processes may sound like familiar routines, yet the critical question that must always be answered is whether your attempts at evading "insanity" have been fruitful.

Most of us have had the tiresome experience of going to great lengths to make changes only to end up stuck back in the mire, right where we started. The reason for this dilemma is that we often do not go deep enough with the implementation of changes. We try a new approach for a few days but end up back where we started because we return to our comfortable ways. In order to effectively change, we need to accurately evaluate our current status and monitor our progress over time. When used correctly, mirrors can be very powerful tools to help us understand ourselves and to hold ourselves accountable for implementing the leadership and management changes we need to make.

Seeing Yourself from Multiple Angles

If you have ever had a suit tailored, you know that a part of the process involves getting up in front of at least three mirrors that, together, provide a semi-panoramic view. Tailors use this configuration so that their customers can see how they look from various angles. It gives them helpful views that they would not otherwise have. There is no arguing with what you see. In fact, you are fortunate to have those multiple angles, and taking the time to examine yourself from each perspective can be an eye-opener.

The same concept applies to the self-assessment of your leadership and management. The use of conceptual mirrors helps to reveal new angles about you that will provide a much more comprehensive view of your management and leadership styles, and the areas that need improvement.

Taking a Humble Self-Assessment

A humble self-assessment is the first step in the process of managing the mirrors. At this stage, you make a conscious effort to see your current habits by looking at a conceptual mirror of the self. Unlike with a physical mirror, you are not going to simply look at your physical appearance. With a conceptual mirror, you should think about your own leadership style and approach to working with your team.

Mentally picture your day at work yesterday and your interactions with the people you work with. Think about the morning routine, dealing with staffing issues, and all of the events throughout the day. Then, answer the following questions:

- What do you see?
- What would you like to improve?
- Are you someone who embraces other people's ideas?
- Were you confident in your decision-making?
- Are you proud or remorseful of your management style?

Continuing with this process of self-reflection, think about when you engage with members of the team and answer the following questions:

- Are you rooted in your own thoughts, or can you be swayed?
- What makes you dig in your heels? What can you do to relax this tendency?

- When was the last time you listened to someone in an honest fashion?
- Do you have faith in your team to do the right thing?
- Are you loved or feared by your team?
- Do you manage with a carrot or a stick?

The questions, when answered truthfully, should provide a very interesting perspective on the underlying emotions you are constantly carrying with you throughout the day. It can also help you to identify areas in which you want to change, develop, and grow.

Looking Over Your Shoulder to See Where You Are

When was the last time you thought about where you *wanted* to be versus where you *actually are*? Using your mental mirror, would the child you were be proud of the person you've become? Would the aspiring practitioner or manager you were at the start of your career be proud of the professional you've become? Consider the following questions:

- Is your relationship with coworkers, patients, and physicians acceptable enough that your former self would be proud of what you have become today?
- If not, what happened? What could you have done differently?
- What should you do different going forward?

These questions can be extremely tough, and answering them can even be painful. But I promise you that it will be worth it to go through each of them and give thoughtful answers. Each one will be another brick laid on the path to self-realization and will contribute to the process of effectively managing what you see in the mirrors.

Getting Comfortable with Your Mirrors: Committing to Daily Reflection

Taking the time to reflect on your management and leadership style is probably going to be a bit uncomfortable initially. But what form of meaningful growth is not somewhat uncomfortable or even perhaps painful? Whether it is learning a new skill or exercising to get to a desired weight goal, you never improve without discomfort. "No pain, no gain," as the saying goes.

That said, I promise that this process gets much easier over time. However, part of the process involves a commitment to taking time at the end of each day to reflect on your daily management and leadership experiences. By doing that, you will find yourself becoming more aware of your actions and the knowledge you will gain, if used properly, can improve your ability to lead the practice.

After a few weeks of dedication to this daily activity, you (and your team) should notice a change. You should be better able to identify triggers that cause you to make rash decisions that are usually the wrong ones and to more easily recognize what it takes to make the right decisions. Over time, you should finally be able to take different actions, experience different results, and stop the "insanity."

CHAPTER 2

The Staff Mirror: Understanding People and Situations

As practitioners and practice managers, one of the most critical job roles that you have is to hold your staff accountable for their actions. In the classic conception of the employer and employee relationship, your staff comes to work, does what is required of them as stated in their job description, and receive remuneration and benefits such as a salary, vacation leave, health insurance (or in-house consultations), and so forth. If only this was how the world works!

In reality, there is a complex interplay between a practice's management and its leadership team, its policies, the staff, the patients, and the wider community in which the practice operates. Accordingly, in this chapter, the idea of managing people and processes will be examined. The importance of knowing your own strengths and shortcomings along with the ability to recognize opportunities for self-improvement will also be examined.

Holding the Practice Accountable

In 1943, Abraham Maslow changed the world of psychology with the publication of *A Theory of Human Motivation*. His "Hierarchy of Needs" proposed several levels of needs that people had to meet before they could achieve self-actualization. Maslow theorized that it is necessary to have your basic physical and psychological needs met before you can reach your full potential.

Every staff member in the practice, including yourself, is at some point along the "Hierarchy of Needs" pyramid. You can apply Maslow's theory to help you become the best possible manager and leader that you can be. By being reminded of the basic psychology of the people you work with, it allows you to tap into their motivations and figure out the best way to move them in the direction you want them to go. Therefore, in this chapter, I will apply this concept to practice management and show you how it can

be used to hold people, including yourself, accountable so that all can enjoy their careers in the practice.

Understanding Your Employees' Needs

As an employer, it is easy—even understandable—to take the stance that your employees are there to meet your needs. After all, you are the one who writes the checks, and it is your staff's responsibility to do the work required of them so that they get their remuneration. I do not necessarily disagree with you in taking this position. However, when you look more closely at Maslow's "Hierarchy of Needs" theory, it should become clear why you need to think a lot more about your employees' needs. If their basic needs are not being met, can they really achieve their highest potential to deliver the best patient experience?

For example, a nurse working in your office may be having problems at home. Perhaps she has a teenager who is using drugs, or her family is facing money problems with a pending eviction or foreclosure. How can any rational human being expect her, or any other person in these types of situations, to be fully attentive in her job, let alone focused on providing the best patient experience? While these scenarios are certainly dramatic, I have learned over the years that they are not as uncommon as you might initially suspect.

Examining Maslow's paradigm can help us see that until the nurse in this scenario can resolve these pressing concerns,

which threaten her very sense of security, she may not be able to fully dedicate herself to her duties in the practice.

Effective managers make it their business to know when their employees are going through rough times. This does not mean digging into their personal lives past the point of professional concern. It just means you should recognize the basic truth that, until any threat to employees' basic needs are resolved, it will be impossible for them to perform at their true potential.

Identifying Red Flags

How can you get to know what's happening with your staff without prying? In my experience, it is quite simple. If the performance level of a team member with a strong record of accomplishment, work ethic, and history of taking the initiative suddenly begins to decline, I know that there is a problem.

The problem will not necessarily be as dire as the ones I described earlier. In fact, in many instances, the problem may be something simple that is occurring within the practice.

Some common examples include:

- A change in the work environment
- Office gossip and a rumor mill "gone wild"
- Problems with management
- Malfunctioning or obsolete technology

The number of items on the list can be very long, but the good news is that if the source of the dysfunction is within the office and within your sphere of influence, you can, as an effective leader, initiate steps to support the employee and hopefully remedy the situation.

Utilizing Constructive Feedback

If you do not have close relationships with your staff members, it is unlikely that they will tell you when their social, safety, or basic needs on Maslow's scale are being threatened. While building the appropriate type of relationship should always be the goal, you can still be an effective leader by keeping a close eye on your team and provide constructive feedback as needed.

For example, let us imagine that one of your nurses is consistently rude to patients. That would give you an opportunity to provide constructive feedback by reminding the nurse of your expectations that courtesy should always be the foundation of every interpersonal relationship.

It would also be your responsibility to address any environmental factors such as gossiping and/or employees frustrated with their broken equipment they are required to use. Failing to address such concerns will most likely lead to two additional problems:

- You run the risk of losing an otherwise qualified employee who, at one point, might have been a good fit for your practice because they see no hope for a positive work environment.

- You may have a situation in which you are perceived as condoning the actions of other staff members that contribute to the lackluster performance of other employees. Over time, these problematic workers will cause colossal damage in your practice.

Mastering the art of providing constructive feedback is always a good investment of your time. However, it is no replacement for forming strong bonds with your staff. If nothing else, this type of connection will help you recognize when an employee is facing the type of problem that needs your attention.

The Situation-Behavior-Impact (SBI) approach provides an effective method for structuring feedback:

1. Define the where and when of the **situation** you're providing feedback on. For example, "This morning when you greeted Ms. Smith at the check out window...."

2. Next, describe the specific **behavior** you want to address. For example, "You took a call on your cell phone while Ms. Smith and her children waited; Ms. Smith's child had just had a vaccination and was fussy..." Make sure to communicate only what you yourself observed as objectively as possible and without subjective judgments or assumptions about what happened and why.

3. The last step is to describe the **impact** on you and /or on the practice. For example, "This meant Ms.

> Smith had to wait several minutes with a fussy child before she could finish checking out. It also meant that our office did not deliver on our promise to always put our patients first."

Your feedback conversation can then take whatever direction you need it to, for example, learning more about why the employee answered the call at that moment (was it an emergency? could it have waited?), reinforcing the rules about no cell phone calls during patient interactions, or coaching the employee through alternative ways to handle emergency calls so that patients aren't left waiting.

Performing Small Acts of Kindness

Years ago, I managed a practice and worked with a pediatrician (Dr. Sara) whom I have always respected. One day, Dr. Sara shared an observation that has stuck with me and greatly impacted how I instruct others to manage their practice.

At this practice, it was customary to throw a farewell lunch whenever an employee was leaving to take a job elsewhere or was retiring. It was a heartfelt gesture, and everyone participated in some way. I thought to myself, "Wasn't it great that they showed so much appreciation for the staff?"

Then Dr. Sara shared her unsolicited perspective with me. She asked, "Why was it that the practice spent more effort and energy saying goodbye to people than they did on trying to keep them in the first place?"

Another example that comes to mind is the fact that my father used to hold an annual Fourth of July get-together for all of the people who worked at his practice. It often involved a zydeco band, moonwalks for the kids, and plenty of amazing dishes prepared by members of the staff. Even if you think some of this may be a bit much, I doubt you would disagree that this type of event helped to strengthen the bonds between everyone who worked in the practice.

I don't mean to suggest that you can only show your appreciation once a year through a grand gesture. Small acts of kindness can be just as effective, maybe even more so, than grand ones. For instance, a gesture of simply bringing in a box of donuts every now and then can go a long way with building goodwill with the staff. Or allowing an employee to leave a little earlier so that the employee can see his child's game or a school play may be well appreciated.

While those are just two examples, you can probably immediately think of 10 or 20 more ways to show your staff that you value their work without breaking the bank.

Every now and then, humanize yourself to your team by ditching the title and making a connection with your staff. The better they understand that you are more than just a boss, the more likely they will be to drop their guard and let you know when a problem is affecting their ability to work (which, in turn, will make you a better boss).

Dealing with Difficult Employees

Earlier in my career, someone told me that they had an employee who consistently refused to show appreciation for such kind gestures. I did not believe it at first and felt they were being cynical. However, I have been involved with practice management long enough that I personally have seen this inexplicable phenomenon firsthand on a repetitive basis. For whatever reason, there are some people who will shun, or spurn, attempts at being kind and thoughtful. When this is the case, this action often involves complaining from the recipient of such kind gesture(s). The individual did not spend a single cent on the donuts you bought, but the individual still moped—in plain sight of everybody, of course—because you did not choose that individual's favorite flavor with sprinkles. Other times, an individual's actions may be more aggressive. The employee may make a dramatic show of refusing your token of appreciation as if they were sitting on the trigger of a bear trap waiting for the opportunity to belittle your token of appreciation. If you've never faced this situation before, it can be difficult to even imagine how you would react appropriately to such behavior.

Back in my early school years, I had a teacher who developed a reputation for strict discipline and an expectation that all students in the class would excel to their highest potential. She had been a nurse on the front lines during World War II and served as a consummate reminder of what living through the Great Depression can do to a person. She frequently told our class that if we ever upset her, she would "march through us like Sherman going through Georgia."

Although it would be years before I even knew who General William Tecumseh Sherman was, the way she said it made it perfectly clear that we should not think of crossing her. I knew it. My classmates knew it. And, most importantly, our parents knew that we knew it.

If an employee rejects or ridicules your efforts to show sincere appreciation, your initial reaction might be to take a page out of my teacher's book and "march through the employee like Sherman went through Georgia." Yet, that would be a huge mistake.

You need to address such situations directly but in a calm and civil manner. The worst thing for a leader's reputation is the perception that the leader will admonish (or even fire) people who offend them, because other employees will worry that they will be the next victim when a simple misunderstanding arises. This kind of perception would be harmful for the practice and could contribute to a toxic work environment.

Instead, you should ask the employee why the employee felt that your gesture was insufficient and then listen carefully to the answer provided. By taking the time to hear the employee's concern respectfully, you will learn more about the employee's perspective and recognize that this is his or her way of getting your attention. You may even learn from the employee's response about other issues within the practice that need tending to. The most important thing to do is to listen more than talk. Much like a teenager who lashes out at his or her parents, the employee's behavior can be a cry for help dealing with issues that the employee is facing.

Accepting Constructive Criticism

Just as you will need to provide employees with constructive criticism periodically, the shoe may end up on the other foot every now and then. If you ask an employee why the employee didn't appreciate your gesture, prepare yourself to hear feedback that you may not necessarily want to accept right away.

While no medical practice can function as a democracy wherein every team member gets an equal vote, it is also important to remember that most dictators end up getting shot. Thus, an effective leader needs to strike a balance—making the decisions that need to be made and also listening to the valuable feedback that employees, coworkers, and professional colleagues can provide, even if that means sifting through any biases, negative judgments, or unhelpful attitudes that may be intertwined with that feedback.

As a practice leader, you must hold yourself accountable and foster an environment in which staff are encouraged to share their thoughts, even when their thoughts are critical. Here is a simple approach you can take within the practice:

- Establish a core set of values that will guide everyone's decision-making processes.

- Set fair rules that govern everyone uniformly.
- Lead by example.
- Provide constructive feedback when people fail to comply with the rules you have set.
- Hold people accountable for their actions.

This is not to say that adopting this approach is something that you will be able to do overnight, but these five steps are really all it takes, in addition to being dedicated to sticking with them.

Accountability Is Appreciated

I know that holding people accountable is not always fun, as you may sometimes feel like the bad guy. The person you are holding accountable may also feel the same way about you. The reality is that as a leader, it is your responsibility to hold people answerable for meeting the responsibilities of their job. That is why it is incredibly important to remember that your entire staff will eventually respect your dedication to accountability if you are consistent and fair.

No one wants to work in an environment with vague rules; nor do they like it when the workplace rules are not enforced uniformly. This type of dynamic leads to uncertainty, which employees hate most of all. It is reasonable to expect some challenges along the way, but if you always remember that your staff values accountability, you will find it much easier to create a relevant framework.

At one practice I consulted with, there were three people responsible for checking patients in and scheduling future appointments after the patient was seen. During the check-in process, the receptionists were expected to verify insurance and any outstanding balances. If the insurance verification showed information that was not consistent with what was in the billing system, the receptionist was expected to take the time to resolve the discrepancies.

While two of the receptionists dutifully did their job, one of them avoided making necessary account corrections at all cost. To make matters worse, she would not even take the time to ask the patient for the copayment. As it turned out, this receptionist simply did not want to engage with the patients in any way. She just wanted to do the minimal amount of work and tell the patients to wait their turn to be seen. While the financial consequences were obvious thanks to her failure to collect copayments, it was frustrating for her two coworkers, who obediently did what was expected of them.

Because the manager of the practice was not an approachable person, the staff never took the time to relay their concerns to her. Over time, the two other receptionists began to grow resentful of their coworker for not doing what she was supposed to do and also of the office manager for not realizing that there was a problem.

When the physician became aware of the situation, he respectfully addressed it head-on by reminding the receptionists of the expectations that came with their jobs. During the process of discussing the issues with them, the physician learned that the office manager was not tending to things as he expected her to, and that the individual at the center of the issue had not been properly trained.

Because of varied training efforts and different options within the computer system to check a patient in, each of the receptionists was following different steps in the process, thus leading to confusion about the most efficient way to move the patients through the registration area. Over the subsequent weeks, the receptionists began to work together to streamline the processes. Their collaboration led to open dialogue with each other, and they began to work together as a team. It was much easier for the receptionists to support each other when they had a standardized process to follow that they all understood than when each receptionist did things her own way.

Connecting with People Can Pay Great Dividends

Being able to connect with people is a critical part of managing the mirrors and impacts how people behave in the practice setting. Taking the time to understand your employees' needs and to really connect with those whom you manage and supervise can provide critical insights into the dynamics of various situations. The net benefit for you as a practice leader is that you will be better able to identify problems before they become a crisis. Additionally, this skill allows the practice's management and leadership to more effectively interact with the team.

CHAPTER 3

The Staff Mirror: Understanding Your Team

Once you have a framework in place for instilling accountability and understanding individual employee's situations, you can hold up a mirror to your team (much like you did to yourself) to better understand the dynamics that impact how people work together. Before you do so, though, you must consider the unique dynamics of the modern workforce and how it will impact the process.

The Generation Gap(s)

Today, most practices are staffed by a blend of employees from two or three generations. The spectrum in a medical practice usually extends from people in their late teens to those well over 60 years old. Also, keep in mind that younger employees have had cell phones all their lives while those in their 50s may have been born before the first cassette tape was invented (1962) or the discovery of the polio vaccine (1953). These varying backgrounds mean that everyone brings to the practice a lifetime of experiences influenced by different human innovation and historical events.

My high school physics teacher used to have a favorite expression: "It's all relative." While the statement is a tongue-in-cheek phrase among those in the study of physics, I believe it is very relevant when looking at the dynamics of human interaction. What some generations consider as acceptable behavior would be abhorred by those from another generation. If you do not believe it, then watch what happens when a 20-something throws away a plate of food in front of anyone who lived through the Great Depression.

To be an effective leader, you need a keen understanding of the backgrounds of people from different generations. This fact is not to be confused with stereotyping, though, which makes simplified assumptions about people's abilities based on their age, gender, or racial or ethnic background. Yet, an effective manager or leader will tap into those diverse backgrounds to find solutions because they value different perspectives. They also recognize that different people must be approached (or engaged with) differently.

For example, according to a study from the IBM Institute for Business Value, 61 percent of Gen Xers believe that it's important for teams to reach a consensus before making a decision. Compare that to 55 percent of millennials and just 39 percent of baby boomers. If you do not understand this reality, your attempts at promoting collaboration among your team may fall flat.

Leading a Team of Individuals

Early in my management career, I made the mistake of managing based on my organizational title. Twenty years later, I am still embarrassed by my total ineptitude as an inexperienced leader. My biggest mistake was assuming that all people, regardless of age or gender, accepted my style of doing things. It was not until years later that I realized how naïve I had been. Since day one, I have strived to become what I *thought* was an effective leader, yet it has been a long and painful process to more deeply understand what an effective leader really is.

What I have learned and always try to put into practice is that every individual is unique. Each person must be approached differently for you to work together. Managers and physicians who insist on trying to rule with an iron fist are most likely to fail. I guarantee it. While many people who insist on that style of leadership still run medical practices today, they do so oblivious of the fact that they are surrounded by people who do not respect them. Although there seems to be a pill for every ailment known, some might say there is nothing to fix that kind of stupidity.

Having seen this approach in action, I find that leaders who rule with an iron fist are in a never-ending cycle of hiring replacement staff. This cycle requires them to focus their energy on hiring and training people to keep the office going instead of developing their teams to achieve their highest potential.

Unfortunately for these "leaders," gone are the days when in response to the command "jump!" the employee can be expected to respond by asking "how high?" Instead, the way forward is for leaders to take the time to get to know the people who work for them. While they don't need to be familiar with every detail about an employee's personal life, it would be prudent to know about their family, social background, and professional goals. Considering that most people spend more time interacting with their coworkers during the week than they do their own families, developing a sense of collegiality, connection, and trust can foster a positive work environment, provided leaders maintain their ability to provide constructive feedback and accountability when needed.

From a leadership perspective, taking the time to really know the people you work with also makes it easier to identify how to harness their best efforts and ideas. Something as simple as asking, "What would you do differently?" is an extremely effective management technique. Unfortunately, if the team member does not trust you, you probably will not get an honest answer.

This strategy can also prove beneficial to the well-being of the practice. In Chapter 1, you were shown some of the channels that can provide insights into the operations of your practice, which will help you understand how the practice is perceived. In many instances, each later generation will have a greater fluency with the various channels, and if this strength is harnessed, the practice will be all the richer for it. While millennials may be most at ease with social media and the Internet, baby boomers may have their hands on the pulse of the community via actual in-person conversations with others. Accordingly, each generation can provide feedback that contribute to the advancement of the practice's mission.

The more you invest in getting to know your team, the more likely each member will open up and allow you to manage and lead. Yet, the more you allow an unspoken barrier to develop between you and your employees, the more your actions will be based on a distorted reality, thus undermining your efforts as a leader.

How to Influence Employees

The good news is that bringing out the best in your employees is not rocket science. Here are the four steps you can follow to achieve this goal:

1. Find out what motivates your employees to succeed.
2. Find out why they work where they do.
3. Tap into their intrinsic motivation.
4. Record your observations and adjust your approach as necessary.

How you treat your employees also matters greatly. Managers should view employees under their supervision as teammates and as human beings who, for the most part, just want to be effective and get paid fairly for the work they do.

One technique I learned many years ago is to take the time to write down why you hired each person to join the team. Specifically, document what skills and attributes he or she possessed that made you think they were a good fit, as well as the intangible qualities you saw in the person. Later on, this record can serve as a reminder if things do not turn out well or as the foundation from which to measure your success in coaching the person along a career path.

Employees are not individuals within a hierarchy of inferior ranking. Rather, they should be viewed as members of a team that is assembled to provide a service to patients. These services can include:

- Nurses taking vitals, giving shots, and supporting the physicians
- Receptionists checking patients in and out
- The billing department processing claims
- The housekeeping department keeping the facilities clean
- Supervisors sharing responsibilities and keeping an eye on operational matters
- Managers recognizing each person's motivation to deliver the best quality care to patients by tapping into their employees' strengths and developing them where they are weak
- Physicians evaluating patients and diagnosing their condition(s)

When you bring people to the realization that they are members of a team who all are moving in the same direction, the subsequent collaboration, and the benefits it produces, are inevitable. This shift in thinking may be a major change for most practices, but the positive results will be dramatic.

Leveraging Individuals to Create a Stronger Whole

This new direction is not to say that everyone is treated equally based on the organizational structure. That would mean that everyone on your team is the same, which is never the case. As we just discussed, everyone has a role to play. By recognizing each employee's individuality, you can also leverage their skills and talents to complement the weaknesses of others while building a successful practice.

A baseball team manager has many options to fill a given position, whether it is a fielder, a baseman or a pitcher. However, it is the skills beyond the immediate need that they look at. For example, the manager considers the ability to hit the ball, to steal bases, work ethic, and overall health of the individual when evaluating the team's human resource capacity. Eventually, he will put together a roster that he hopes will lead the team to the World Series.

While there are rules limiting the number of players that can be on the field at one time, the manager learns how to maximize the team's performance within the confines of the rules. Similarly, the financial realities of a medical practice place limits on how many people you can hire. Therefore, it is important to look for people who can fill the roles needed. To do so effectively, you must look beyond the individual job you are looking to fill.

For example, if you are looking to fill a receptionist position, why not hire a Medical Assistant? In a typical Medical Assistant training program, the students are taught the intricacies of being a receptionist as well as clinical skills. Hiring such an individual brings a skill set that could be used beyond the position you are looking to fill at some point in the future. Having an individual who can serve in a dual role within the office is not just a technique to have a cadre of people who have multiple skills but also a smart money-saving strategy.

Agreement, Compromise, and Consent

At this point in the chapter, you have learned to look at your team from several different angles. Hopefully, you have also already begun to formulate some valuable insights about how you can help your team better serve your practice.

Before we conclude this chapter, let us look at the three most common methods for moving a practice forward.

- **Agreement**—A situation in which all the decision makers come to the same decision about a course of action.

- **Compromise**—A state in which all team members work toward an agreement by sacrificing some of their initial aims (e.g., "I will do ABC, if you do XYZ")
- **Consent**—A point when decision makers do not all agree on a plan but do agree to follow and publicly support the decision of the group

In a perfect world, practice leaders would reach agreement all the time. Compromise could be dangerous because it sometimes forces one person to do something that he or she does not think is in the best interest of the practice in order for a certain action to be fulfilled. However, until then, consent must be an option or the practice will never move forward. The trick with providing consent is that while individual decision makers may not agree with the action to be taken, they provide support for it in both word and deed.

Meanwhile, caution should be taken when a decision is made but leadership is not unified in supporting the final decision. I once worked with a practice that experienced significant financial hardship. While some of the physicians were opposed to giving a Christmas bonus, others felt the need to do so. The reality was that there was simply no cash on hand to pay the employees a bonus. The decision was made to defer the annual bonus to the middle of the following year if the following specific objectives were attained:

1. Patient satisfaction survey results on the practice's website had to increase by 10 percent.

2. The percent of well-child visits had to exceed 30 percent.
3. The percent of patients utilizing the patient portal had to double.

There were various reasons for these specific goals. Patient satisfaction had deteriorated recently, and it was important that the practice take steps to improve this vital metric. The percent of well-child visits needed to increase also since that was a source of "easy money" in pediatrics. Additionally, the number of patients using the patient portal was essential to ensuring *Meaningful Use* compliance.

Most importantly, the six-month delay allowed the physicians to budget for the bonus expense. If the goals were attained, the financial condition would naturally improve at the same time, thus allowing the practice to afford giving the employees a bonus. Sadly, what happened next led to more problems.

A few of the physicians decided to support the decision, while others grossly undermined the effort by not showing a united front. Instead of speaking as one voice to the employees, a few of the physicians decided to share with the employees that they had voted to give bonuses and named the physicians who had voted not to give bonuses. As a result, there was great turmoil within the practice and the ensuing furor ended up driving a wedge between the physicians and the staff.

Instead of supporting the collective decision, a few of the physicians tried to curry favor with the employees at the expense of their professional relationships. Basically, instead of behaving as leaders of the practice, these rogue physicians had succumbed to the pressure of forming cliques and not respecting their role and responsibility as part of the leadership of the practice.

CHAPTER 4

The Boss's Mirror: Managing Up and Sometimes Sideways

At this point, you should have a much better idea of what it takes to manage the people your practice employs. Unfortunately, if you have an employer or a business partner, you do not have complete control over management decisions. Worse yet, these people may not always be receptive to change. They may even become angry or irritated over the simplest issues, making a leader's job that much harder. All is not lost, though, as a few simple techniques can be helpful in creating a positive environment at the practice.

"Can You Help Me Understand?"

My mother's knack for talking with people provides a great lesson that can set the stage for discussion and better understanding. Aside from being the mother of five children, being a grandmother to 19 children, having a doctorate in divinity, and being a church organist for over 40 years, my mother is also a registered nurse and currently serving as the

Paul D. Vanchiere, MBA

Director of Palliative Care and Chairperson of the Ethics Committee for a hospital.

In her current role, she manages to do the impossible:

- Helping families tend to the needs of relatives who are in end-of-life situations
- Ensuring that the patients' wishes are honored
- Being mindful of the fiscal responsibilities of a hospital
- Navigating the sometimes competing concerns of patients, families, and physicians
- Reviewing quality and ethics concerns within the hospital
- Ensuring that all decisions are consistent with the hospital's Catholic values and mission

One thing I have often heard my mother say throughout the years is, "Can you help me understand?" Regrettably, it was not until a few years ago that I finally realized the impact of that simple five-word question. When asked sincerely, the power of that question is amazing!

Since realizing the potential of that short question, I use it repeatedly when I visit clients around the country to assess their practices. When used appropriately (and sincerely), it has never failed to start a dialogue and help me better understand another person's perspective.

The beauty of this question is that it can be a non-confrontational way to get to the bottom of an issue. It can result in someone sharing details that leads to a resolution when the dynamics of the relationship would otherwise not allow for a candid conversation. Another benefit of this technique is that the approach dovetails very nicely with the idea that working together to decide a course of action is more important than implementing a bad idea proffered by the most dominant person involved in the discussion.

Keeping the Lines of Communication Open

My mother also believes that when people stop talking to each other, they stop working toward finding a solution to the problem at hand. Here, again, she's right.

Once you understand another person's point of view a little better, you, as the listener, can identify the person's concerns. That, in turn, will allow you to see the true motivation behind the potential conflict and to identify ways to address the person's concerns constructively. This all hinges on opening the lines of communication instead of shutting them down out of frustration or other reactions.

As a manager or leader, when you stop communicating with your team members, they are no longer sharing ideas with you and providing feedback, a situation that completely undermines effective leadership. Similarly, when you report to a higher up who has decision-making authority or you have colleagues who share decision-making authority over your practice, eliciting their concerns and keeping open the lines of communication can work as a powerful two-part approach to building trust, bridging divides, and forming consensus.

Paul D. Vanchiere, MBA

The Responsibility and Challenge of Helping Your Boss Look in the Mirror

By providing feedback to your boss, you allow him or her to gain information with which to make decisions for the practice. Many of you see this as part of your core responsibilities in managing a practice, but at times, it is not an easy task. While some bosses are open to trusted employees who help them to see the land mines and avoid pitfalls, others seem to want to be surrounded by yes-people who support their ideas and decisions without question. This can put you in the challenging position of having information that is important for your boss to know but that she or he may not want to hear.

With the knowledge that you have from reading this book and doing the exercises on the ManagingTheMirrors.com website, you are in a favorable position to help your boss to look in the mirror and manage the reflection that she or he sees there. Sharing some of the concepts and strategies in this book can be a way to open up a dialogue that puts you in a better position to gain trust and to help your boss make better-informed decisions.

These same dynamics—and opportunities—are at play if you share practice management responsibilities with partners.

So, above all else, make sure you facilitate communication by "managing up" with those above you, and "managing sideways" with your partners. It may not always be easy, but it will always be necessary if your practice is to succeed.

CHAPTER 5

The Practice's Mirror

At this stage, you can finally begin holding up a mirror to your practice. In many ways, the practice's reflection in the mirror will be a summation of all the other components that we have covered thus far: you, your team, and those above you.

If you stopped reading right now and *only* focused on the previous chapters, you would see major improvements in your practice. However, taking the time to get a comprehensive perspective on your entire operation in addition will pay big dividends.

How to Develop the Right Culture in Your Practice

In recent years, a lot has been said about the importance of cultivating the right culture in a practice. The conventional advice seems to be that businesses should spare no expense to make certain that their culture is taught to every employee, often through holding multiple workshops or courses within a year.

This kind of massive undertaking could cost your practice a lot of time and money. I am happy to report, though, that they are completely unnecessary. Following is the easy, inexpensive way to cultivate the culture you want in your practice.

1. **Create a Mission Statement and Guiding Principles**

   The practice should develop a mission statement and guiding principles that are posted visibly and are emphasized often to all staff.

2. **Teach the Desired Culture**

   Based on the organization's mission and objectives, make sure all staff know what is expected of them. Whether it is through a Patient's Bill of Rights or giving employees instructions on the proper way to handle a telephone call about a physician's availability, expectations about the culture of the practice must be introduced and reinforced at every opportunity.

3. **Live the Culture**

   Think about how you want your staff to act and then emulate that ideal, day in and day out. As a leader, you set the tone for your practice. Do not expect employees to operate at a higher level than you do.

4. **Measure Success**

   By deciding on the desired culture, the practice will be able to measure the movement toward that goal. While there might not be hard data like lab tests to determine exactly what the progress is, qualitative approaches to measuring success work just as well.

5. **Reward Good Behaviors**

   Be on the lookout for the kind of behaviors that you want to promote in your practice. Positive reinforcement is a powerful tool, especially when you draw attention to it. Furthermore, if all you do is punish people, it will seem like there is no pleasing you. Preempt this kind of negative impression by demonstrating that there are all kinds of ways in which employees can earn your praise.

The Importance of a Mission and Values:

You will make things a lot easier on yourself if you first establish your practice's mission and values. This will help serve to solidify the standards that you have for your employees. One of my closest friends, Brandon Betancourt, an MBA graduate from the Chicago area, embodies this concept. He readily focuses on values *instead* of rules of conduct, which is where the vast majority of leaders put their attention.

He shared with me that it is not possible to make rules for every situation. Instead, give your team values to which they must adhere during the day. Encourage them to follow these ideals and bring the employee(s) back in line when they go off the path.

These standards do not have to be complicated, either. If you get too specific with them, they will soon resemble the long list of rules you are trying to avoid. One example of a very simplistic value that I adhere to is this: "If you do what is best for the patient, you can never go wrong." I truly believe—and have seen proof—that if employees adopt this value and act in accordance with it, then patients will have a superior experience with your practice.

Hiring for Your Practice Culture

Establishing clear values for your practice and encouraging employees to adopt them will take a bit of work initially, though it will certainly pay off in the future. Going forward, be sure to hire people who will support the culture that you want at your practice. Otherwise, you may find that each new employee will set your efforts back instead of helping them move forward.

The following are some pointers to keep in mind so that your hiring practices will be much more effective.

Hire for Attitude and Train for Talent

Many have heard the overly used phrase, "Hire for attitude and train for talent." Simply put, the idea is that you can teach most people the skills they need, but the right attitude is nearly impossible to teach. In the medical profession, I understand it is not exactly this simple. Many of your employees need specific credentials that you cannot make up for with any amount of on-the-job training. However, if those foundational requirements are met, I implore you to look for people who share your practice's values, and where you have the opportunity to train for talent, make sure you hire individuals who have an attitude that is consistent with the culture and values of your practice. If you hire people who need constant reminders, you are going to micromanage yourself to an early grave.

Let People in Positions of Responsibility Do Their Job

Micromanaging a member of the team is one of the biggest pitfalls a leader can run into because it simply sucks the life out of people on both sides of the equation. It leaves one team member feeling like he or she can never do anything right and the leader like he or she needs to continually follow up with the team member, thus distracting both of them from concentrating on their core responsibilities. Where this situation commonly occurs is when the physician hires a manager or administrator but does not give the manager or administrator the authority to make decisions. This lack of authority leads to the need to micromanage the person(s) involved and results in a few things happening:

1. **The manager feels powerless and loses confidence in the ability to lead**. The physician needs to trust the people hired to do the job. If there is a lack of

trust, then the practice should consider personnel changes after carefully evaluating the root cause of the manager's not meeting the physician's expectations.

2. **The team members lose respect for the manager because they do know who the real boss is**. If they have no respect for the manager, the team members will continually involve the physician in every decision, which is contrary to the reason the manager was hired.

When You Have Great Talent, Get Out of the Way

Throughout my childhood, my siblings and I worked at my father's practice in various capacities. These experiences gave me a front-row seat from which to learn all about the dynamics of health care at a very young age. By the time I finished school, my dad's practice was made up of eight providers seeing patients at three locations. During the subsequent three years, the practice grew to 18 providers in eight locations. Clearly, they were doing something right.

One of the most important things I learned from my father was to hire the right people and give them the space they needed to do their job. Often I work with clients who have great talent on their team, but the physicians cannot help but meddle in every decision being made, thereby undermining the leadership structure needed within a practice. Physicians need to trust the people they hire to do the job they were hired to do instead of micromanaging them.

In my father's practice, Cheryl was a Registered Nurse and worked in the practice for over 20 years. Over the years, her position evolved from direct patient care to mostly managerial duties. One of her roles was to keep the peace among the staff. I believe that at some point along the way, my father realized that there were certain things that were best handled by Cheryl. This freed him up to see patients and to manage the practice's finances.

Cheryl had a knack for talking with people, getting them to calm down while seeking to understand the root of their problem. Her great interpersonal skills were an asset that my father cherished in the practice. Since there were 18 providers in eight locations, along with many employees, Buzzy made a conscious effort to trust Cheryl in her decision making.

My father trusted her judgment, and from my perspective, he did not micromanage her. In the rare instance when he disagreed with her actions, he would talk to her privately about his concerns. Doing so allowed him the opportunity to understand her perspectives on an issue while being able to coach her in some way. Their mutual respect fostered a high level of trust in each other. This trust is the foundation of leadership, and without it, leaders resort to micromanagement to compensate.

Trusting other members of the team does not happen overnight. With Cheryl, she had been a nurse for many years, and as the practice grew, she assumed more responsibilities. The responsibilities grew as her skill set enlarged, and my father trusted her increasingly over time. Trust doesn't happen overnight, but it can be cultivated.

Finding the Right Fit: Cultivating Leaders from Within vs. Hiring External Candidates

There has been a tendency among many of my clients to "hire an MBA" to join the practice, as if every newly minted MBA has the right attitude and decision-making ability to do the job. Don't get me wrong: I'm an MBA. I *like* MBAs.

The reality is that the most successful practices I work with have leaders and managers who have worked their way up to their current positions. This process takes years but allows physicians to understand individuals' values and work ethic. Like a successful marriage, the relationships evolve over time as everyone understands and appreciates each other's strengths and weaknesses.

Sometimes an employee comes into the practice in one role and forever is cast in that role. As a good leader, you should challenge yourself to continually explore the depth of all team members' abilities, in order to identify opportunities to expand their skill-skills and to leverage them to fill the practice's needs.

One practice with which I was consulting previously had hired a receptionist. While this person dutifully did her job, she seemed to grasp the big picture and wanted to assume more responsibility, like helping with subspecialty referrals. For some reason, the practice manager could not see past the individual's desire to contribute to the practice in a more meaningful way or recognize the fact that she was organized enough to assume this important role.

When I became aware of the need for a referral coordinator and the receptionist's desire to move into that role, I fought tooth and nail to make it happen because I was so convinced that the receptionist had the right attitude and work ethic. The initial reply from the manager was that the receptionist did not know how to do the job. My immediate response was to ask the manager if she was willing to teach the receptionist what she needed to know. Even though taking the time to hire someone "fresh off the street" would have taken considerable time and would require more resources to train them, the practice manager could not see the receptionist's potential to quickly fill an urgent need.

This is the trap that you can sometimes fall into when you fail to explore the depth of your team members' abilities or to exert a bit of creativity to find a way to satisfy the needs of the practice and the desires of the employees.

For the practices that have a need to fill a leadership position but that do not have anyone within the practice who can be promoted, they need to be very careful in their quest to find the "perfect" person to fill the role. Here again, prioritizing attitude and cultural fit in the hiring process as you choose between qualified candidates sets you on the path for a successful hire.

How My Dad Brought the Right People Together

My father did not end up surrounded by such talented, driven people by accident. Instead, it happened because of several factors that brought such skilled individuals together. Each person hired:

- Was looking for work when a need for their skills presented itself in the practice
- Brought to the practice an exemplary work ethic that, in turn, brought out the best in others
- Had the right skills but also, more importantly, the right personality, which enriched the entire patient experience

A trip I took to Walmart with my father when I was a teenager really drives this point home. After we picked up what we needed, we headed to the checkout. There, I noticed my dad intently focused on what the cashier was doing. Interestingly, he was not focused on her technical job (scanning and bagging the items) but was rather taken by her interactions with the customers. She was personable and engaged with the customers in a positive manner.

Later, after we loaded everything into his suburban, my father shared his thoughts on the experience:

- He noticed that the person checking us out had the requisite skills to do her job.
- She did not have to do anything more than scan the items, take the customers' money, and provide change.
- She *chose* to engage with the customers; it obviously was not a requirement of the job, something that the cashiers in other lanes made perfectly clear.

- Her motivation to engage with the customers changed the dynamics of a mundane process into one that was pleasant and positive.
- Whether she was doing this to help pass the time or because she was genuinely interested in the customers really had no bearing on the process; regardless of her motivation, the customers had a positive experience, and it likely made her job more enjoyable.

My father then told me that he had offered her a job while she was bagging the things we bought. He told me that he wanted her to work for him because of the simple fact that, if she could find a way to make the best of a mundane position, she would be a great addition to the team of receptionists at the practice.

When I expressed concern about whether she would know what to do, he assured me that people with the right personality and basic clerical skills can be trained for the position he had in mind. Obviously, she did not have the skills to be a nurse, but my father wasn't thinking about that. Rather, he saw the potential in someone and thought about the best position for her on his team.

CHAPTER 6

The Patients' Experience as a Mirror for Your Practice

Finally, let us cover the most important variable in the entire equation: the patient. At the end of the day, the success of your practice will depend entirely on how well you have served your patients. Everything else will be for nothing if you lose sight of this principle.

Like the experience in the boutique that was referenced previously where multiple mirrors allow you to see your new suit or dress from various angles, the practice needs to examine itself periodically from multiple angles to see how it is perceived by the patients being served. You, as a practice leader, should ask yourself, "Would I want to be a patient in this practice?"

What's the State of Your Office?

When was the last time you looked around your office? When I ask most people this question, their honest answer is that they cannot remember the last time they made an effort to look at their physical surroundings to get a real sense of its condition. This situation is largely understandable because everyone is busy these days, especially those who must manage an entire practice. There is no end to the obligations that demand one's time.

During a stint as a manager for a pediatric practice, I was approached by a patient's mother and told about a dirty Kleenex in the waiting room. This mother took the time to explain to me that she was appalled by the state of uncleanliness of the waiting room,-especially in the middle of the flu season. What made this situation particularly problematic was that she had seen the same Kleenex tucked in a corner of the waiting room during a prior visit a week earlier.

Embarrassed, I assured the mother that such a find was not what the practice expected to happen and that I would follow up on the situation. After discarding the Kleenex, I shared the mother's feedback with the team. While sharing the story, it became obvious that the cleanliness of the office had recently deteriorated.

After a bit of digging, I learned that the company contracted to provide janitorial services had made some personnel changes the previous month. Admittedly, I had become so accustomed to peripherally scanning the office for such issues throughout the course of my day that I did not take the time to look at the practice from the patient's point of view. Had I, as a leader in the practice, taken the time to walk through the office with the perspective of the patient, I might have noticed the Kleenex and avoided an embarrassing situation.

Still, if you are dedicated to becoming a better manager, you need to find time to pause and try, as best you can, to look at your practice from the patient's point of view.

Eliciting Patient Perspectives

One practice I worked with recently had a group of mothers who would occasionally meet at the office to share their ideas and listen to future office plans. While such an endeavor brought with it many marketing opportunities that we could discuss at length, the point is that the practice was not afraid to ask the harshest critics for feedback. Fortunately for the practice, the staff had the fortitude to make the commitment to hearing the truth.

More importantly, they sincerely appreciated the feedback, did everything possible to implement the good ideas, and helped the mothers understand why the bad ideas would not work. Since the dialogue was so effective, the practice was able to help parents understand why certain things were done the way they were done. The collateral benefit was that this feedback allowed the practice to better understand the expectations of the patients.

Because of this effort, the practice changed many things, including the following:

1. It began to start seeing patients on a walk-in basis starting at 7:00 each morning. This allowed many dual-working families the opportunity to have their child seen before going to work. This clearly was a situation in

which the practice responded to the changing needs of the marketplace. Interestingly, there was one physician who was interested in starting work earlier so that she could be home sooner to pick up her young children after school, so the practice created a real "win-win" situation.

2.   It realized that patients wanted the flexibility of choosing to have checkups for their children during weekend hours. Again, because there were many dual-working families, the families wanted to have their child followed by their pediatrician without having to take time away from work. These changes allowed the children to receive the care they needed while providing the practice with some guaranteed income during weekend hours.

What a Grocery Store Taught Me about Handling Patient Complaints

Several years ago, I made a late-night run to the grocery store to grab a few essentials. As I was putting things on the conveyor belt at the checkout, I noticed an "interesting" pattern of what appeared to be remnants of items that had previously passed through the checkout area. Having lived in a fraternity house in New Orleans during college and being a bachelor until after the age of 30, I have seen and tolerated many yucky things. Still, I was completely grossed out by what I saw. To avoid placing my milk on top of any wet spots that might have been left by raw meat and which would eventually make its way into my refrigerator with fresh food, I carefully placed the milk container on the conveyor belt in a "safe" place.

On my way out, I extended my usual courtesies to the security guard, Leone. Over the years, I had come to know him well, thanks to my many late-night runs to get supplies for my three daughters. For some reason, the entire checkout process disturbed me to the point that I felt compelled to say something, so I shared my observations with him. Although Leone was not in any way responsible for the source of my concerns, he took the time to listen. Then, he offered a series of profound comments that immediately changed the way I train clients about customer service.

After listening to me in a respectful manner and showing empathy for my concerns, the first words out of his mouth were an explanation of "what's supposed to happen." He then went on to offer me his understanding of the expectations placed on the cashiers with regard to keeping the conveyor belts clean. For a few days, I thought about how Leone handled my concern. Leone's approach to me, as a customer, legitimized my concerns, and he took the extra step to share with me the standards of the grocery store in a way that provided assurance of the company's commitment to an excellent customer experience.

Sadly, I often hear from medical staff members about how physicians and managers pass blame off onto them. The common thread is that these "leaders" feel the need to project some sense of authority in front of the patients to satisfy their own egos. What normally ends up happening is that the patients lose respect for the employees involved, the employees are hurt, and the physicians or managers pump up their false sense of self-worth while further convincing themselves that the employees are not worthy of trust and respect. This situation is not supposed to occur.

What Is Supposed to Happen

Over the past several years, I have told the preceding story to physicians and managers as a way of conveying a better way to address patient complaints. Prefacing answers with "What is supposed to happen" accomplishes several important things:

- It validates the patient's concern
- It assures the patients that any negative experiences they had *are not* standard for the practice.
- It keeps the physicians and/or managers from saying anything unprofessional.
- It avoids automatically casting any employees involved in an unfavorable light with the patients.
- It provides the patients with reassurance that the issue will be addressed.

For this approach to work, however, managers and physicians need to take the time to address patients' complaints in a rational manner. More importantly, managers and physicians must be patient enough to take the time to investigate what happened. Lastly, following my mother's advice, it is helpful for managers and physicians to engage with the employees involved by starting with the "can you help me understand" question so that they can find the root cause of the potential problem. Too often physicians and managers go into such conversations with guns blazing, positive that they know what happened, they know who is to blame, and they know what needs to happen next to avoid the situation occurring in the future, when, in fact, they don't have the full picture.

If physicians and managers must repeatedly address the same issues with the same employees, then corrective measures may be necessary. For single instances of patient complaints, though, care must be taken to investigate such issues delicately. Remember, the person making the complaint is providing feedback that is important for the practice to see and understand. But taking the time also to hear the employee's perspective can help make sure that managers and physicians have a "full-mirror" view of the situation.

The worst thing that can happen is that a leader does not hear any complaints at all, because I strongly believe that complaints are good for the practice. Without complaints, leaders will never improve their practice and possibly will fade into irrelevance.

Complaints should be viewed as "opportunities to improve." They should be embraced to help leaders realize where they need to develop the team, improve processes, or make personnel changes.

A FINAL THOUGHT ABOUT MANAGING THE MIRRORS

In a typical pediatric practice, as many as 20-30 children per physician may be seen each day. Each of these children will have at least one adult with them and perhaps even a sibling or two. As these people move in and out of your practice, it is important to realize that they are the reason you have a job. Without them, there would be no need for a medical practice.

If you are going to provide the best possible care to patients, physicians and practice managers cannot do it alone. A successful medical practice requires many different people, working as part of a team, to meet the needs of patients, and that team needs good leadership. The entire philosophy I have presented in this book is the result of years of real-world experience, dating back to my childhood when I observed my father in his practice. What is most clear to me—and I hope I've shared it clearly with you—is that effective leadership can be attained by:

- **Managing Your Own Mirror for Self-Improvement**
  This is probably the most obvious benefit of using a mental mirror. It gives you an opportunity to objectively assess your current talents and aptitude as a manager and to chart a course for growth.

- **Managing Your Team's Mirrors**

  This is critical so that you can provide feedback about the gap between the expectations placed upon your team and the realities of their job performance.

- **Managing the Mirrors of the Practice**

  Ensuring that the people you hire onto the team are constantly reminded of the values that your practice embraces is critical. If as a leader you neglect the culture, the practice will surely fail. If as a leader you nurture the culture, your practice will be successful beyond your highest expectations.

As you continue your leadership journey, I hope the insights that I have shared in this book will provide you with practical tools and guidance to help you and your practice flourish.

ABOUT THE AUTHOR

With over 20 years of healthcare management and finance experience, Paul has worked with physicians specializing in pediatrics, cardiology and pathology practices. Combined with his experience working for a physician-owned health network and his involvement with physician practice acquisitions for one of the largest not-for-profit hospital networks in Texas, Paul has a unique perspective on healthcare. He specializes in completing a comprehensive set of financial analyses, including practice cost, physician compensation, and managed care contract negotiations.

Paul founded the Pediatric Management Institute to provide an array of services for pediatric practices of all sizes, focusing on financial and operational issues. He is involved in a variety of advocacy efforts related to ensuring access to healthcare and education for children with special needs.

Paul is married to Laura Williamson Vanchiere, and they have three daughters, Anna Beth, Camille and Eloise.

Printed in the United States
By Bookmasters